DO YOU REALLY WANT

TO VISIT A DESERT?

WRITTEN BY BRIDGET HEOS · ILLUSTRATED BY DANIELE FABBRI

Amicus Illustrated is published by Amicus
P.O. Box 1329, Mankato, MN 56002
www.amicuspublishing.us

Library of Congress Cataloging-in-Publication Data
Heos, Bridget, author.
 Do you really want to visit a desert? / by Bridget Heos ;
illustrated by Daniele Fabbri. — First edition.
    pages cm. — (Do you really want to visit...?)
 Audience: K-3.
 Summary: "A child goes on an adventure in the Great
Basin desert, learning about the climate, and encountering
animals and plants that live in the desert biome. Includes
world map of deserts and glossary"— Provided by
publisher.
 Includes bibliographical references.
 ISBN 978-1-60753-450-1 (library binding) —
ISBN 978-1-60753-665-9 (ebook)
 1. Desert ecology—Juvenile literature. 2. Deserts—
Juvenile literature. I. Fabbri, Daniele, 1978- ill. II. Title.
III. Series: Do you really want to visit—?
 QH541.5.D4H46 2015
 577.54—dc23   2013028433

Editor: Rebecca Glaser
Designer: Kathleen Petelinsek

Printed in the United States of America at
Corporate Graphics in North Mankato, Minnesota.
10 9 8 7 6 5 4 3 2

ABOUT THE AUTHOR

Bridget Heos is the author of more than 60 books for
children, including many Amicus Illustrated titles and
her recent picture book *Mustache Baby* (Houghton
Mifflin Harcourt, 2013). She lives on the prairie of
Kansas City with her husband and four children.

ABOUT THE ILLUSTRATOR

Daniele Fabbri was born in Ravenna, Italy, in 1978.
He graduated from Istituto Europeo di Design in Milan,
Italy, and started his career as a cartoon animator,
storyboarder, and background designer for animated
series. He has worked as a freelance illustrator since
2003, collaborating with international publishers and
advertising agencies.

So you want to visit the desert? Sure, the desert is beautiful.
But conditions are harsh. Could you survive?

You'd better start packing! You will need a hat and sunscreen. But you WON'T need an umbrella. Deserts get less than 10 inches (25 cm) of rain per year.

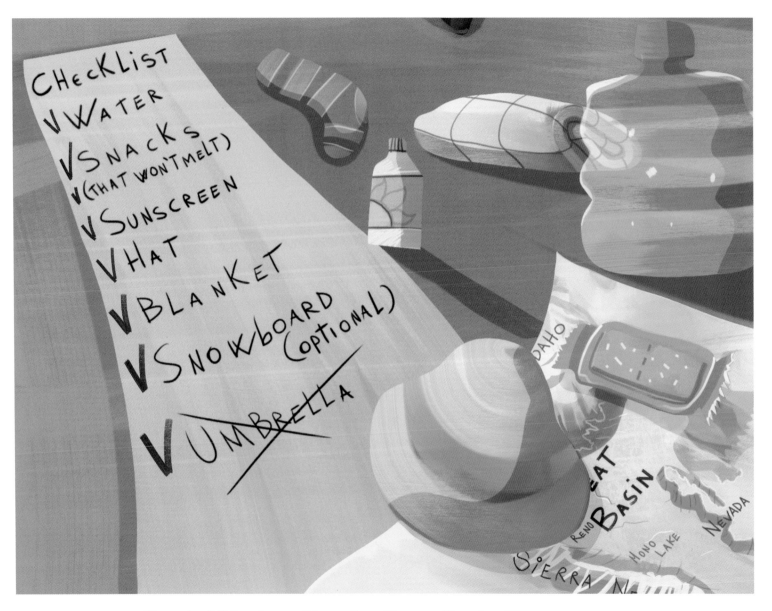

Ready? You're off to the Great Basin Desert.
The largest desert in America, it has sand dunes,
mountains, rivers, and strange rock formations.

First stop is the Fiery Furnace. Wind and ice eroded these rocks long ago. It's a maze of arches and canyons. Good thing you have a guide.

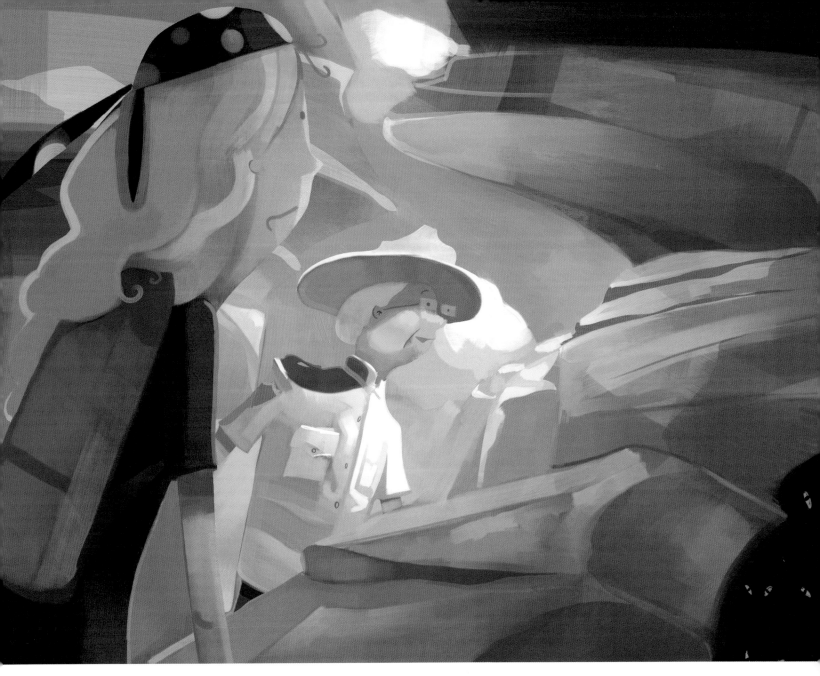

The canyons can be a tight squeeze! But the shade feels nice on this 99°F (37.2°C) day. Be careful! Other animals seek shelter in the shade, too.

If you see a rattlesnake, stay calm. Back away.

Avoid piles of rocks, where a venomous scorpion could be hiding ...

. . . from a Western Whiptail lizard, which eats scorpions.

Are you hungry? How about a snack break? Ouch! Don't sit there!

It's a cactus. It survives the desert by storing water in its stem.
The spikes protect the cactus from animals that want to eat it.

The animals can snack on the fruit and flowers, though.

Animals must adapt to the dry desert, too. Beneath you lives a kangaroo rat that drinks no water at all. It does not sweat. Its urine is solid. It stays cool underground during the day.

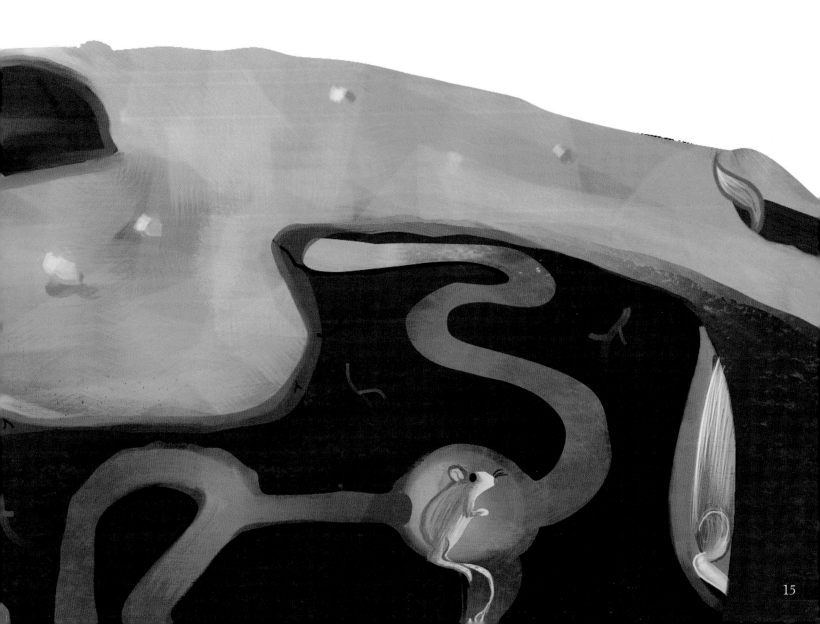

You do sweat. You must keep drinking water. Uh-oh. You may have heard that you can get water from a cactus. But it tastes gross and could make you sick.

If you really need water . . .

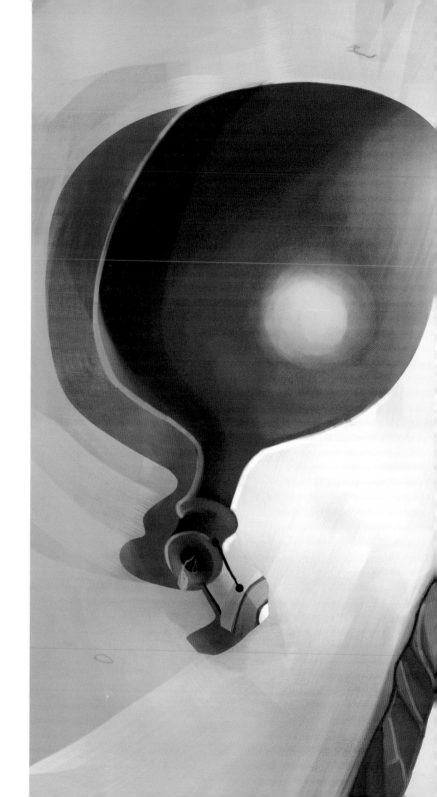

. . . you have to find a river. Be careful of the
sand beside water. It could be quicksand!

If you step in quicksand, lay on your side. Slowly pull one leg out at a time. Now, army-crawl across the sand. Phew!

You should find sand that is safer to walk on—or to snowboard down! Yee haw! These dunes are called the Little Sahara.

It's getting late. The desert gets cold at night. Good
thing you have your blanket. Good night, desert!

TEN LARGEST DESERTS OF THE WORLD

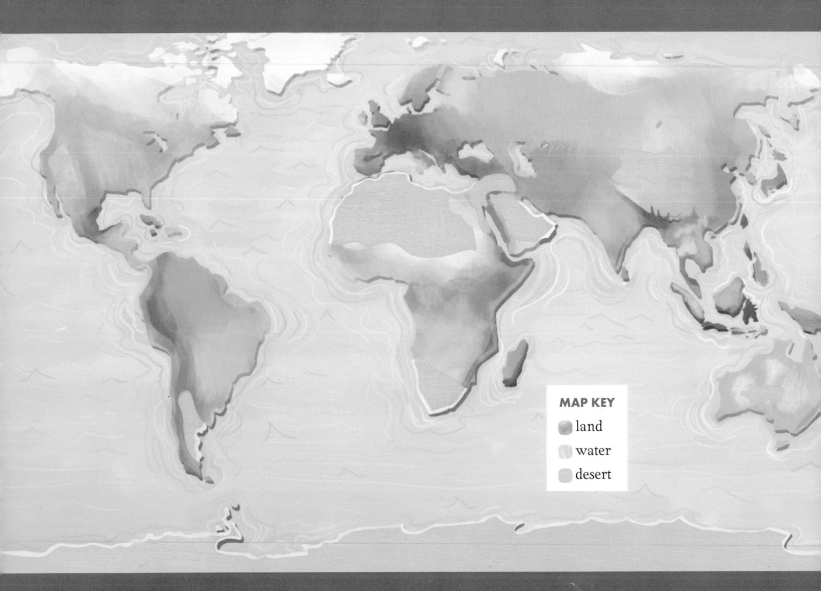

MAP KEY

land

water

desert

PROTECT THE DESERT

Global warming and population growth could make deserts hotter and drier. To help protect deserts you can:

- Walk or bike whenever possible. Fossil fuels from cars add to global warming. Extra heat can destroy desert biomes.

- Don't leave water running.

- For your yard, choose native plants, which can rely on rainwater and don't need extra watering. This conserves water in deserts, or wherever you live.

GLOSSARY

adapt To develop special behaviors or body features in order to survive an environment.

desert A land area that receives less than 10 inches (25 cm) of precipitation per year.

dune A mound of sand formed by wind or water.

erode To gradually wear away, usually from water, wind, or ice.

quicksand Any wet sand in which a heavy object or living thing will sink.

venomous Being able to inject venom or poison into another creature, for example with fangs or a stinger.

READ MORE

Benoit, Peter. **Deserts**. A True Book. New York: Children's Press, 2011.

Lundgren, Julie K. Desert Dinners: Studying Food Webs in the Desert. Vero Beach, Fla.: Rourke Pub., 2009.

Newland, Sonya. Desert Animals. Saving Wildlife. Mankato, Minn.: Smart Apple Media, 2012.

Rabe, Tish. **Why Oh Why Are Deserts Dry?** New York: Random House, 2011.

WEBSITES

Deserts—Great Basin National Park
http://www.nps.gov/grba/naturescience/deserts.htm
Read about the how Great Basin Desert was formed and what you can see if you visit this park in Nevada.

Deserts—Kids Geography Videos, Games, and Lessons
http://www.neok12.com/Deserts.htm
This site has facts and games about deserts, but the best part is the videos showing desert wildlife and climate.

Kangaroo Rat Fact Sheet
http://www.desertmuseum.org/kids/oz/long-fact-sheets/krat.php
Learn more about the Kangaroo Rat and how it has adapted to live in the desert.

What's it Like Where You Live?: Desert Topics
http://www.mbgnet.net/sets/desert/
View photos and read descriptions of desert plant and animal life.